SMART BRAIN RIGHT BRAIN

# Basic Arithmetic

Om KIDZ
An imprint of Om Books International

First Published in 2021 by

Om Kidz | Om Books International

**Corporate & Editorial Office**
A-12, Sector 64, Noida 201 301
Uttar Pradesh, India
Phone: +91 120 477 4100
Email: editorial@ombooks.com
Website: www.ombooksinternational.com

**Sales Office**
107, Ansari Road, Darya Ganj
New Delhi 110 002, India
Phone: +91 11 4000 9000
Email: sales@ombooks.com


Author: Shweta Sinha
Editor: Kirti Pathak
Art & Design: Anshuman Pandey, Gaurav Bhandari, Harish Arya

ISBN: 978-93-5276-855-4

Printed in India

10 9 8 7 6 5 4 3 2 1

# CONTENTS

# 1. One More

It was Lucy's birthday. She invited all her friends and family for her birthday party. She received many gifts. Can you count them for her?

5 gifts

Lucy received 5 gifts from her party guests.

Lucy's cousin Alicia came in late. She brought Lucy 1 more gift. Now can you count how many gifts Lucy has got?

5 gifts. 1 more gift.

1 more than 5 is 6.
Lucy now has 6 gifts.

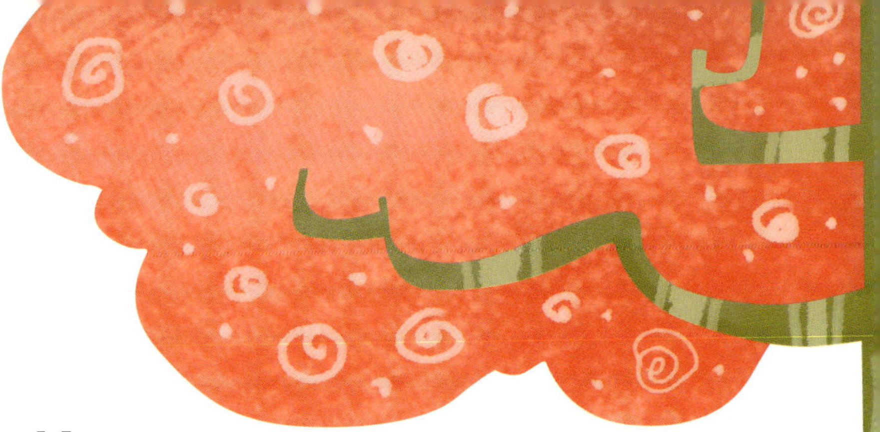

# Two More

Mommy squirrel has been working hard to collect acorns for the winter. But, Mommy squirrel forgot how many she has collected. Can you help her count them?

8

acorns

Mommy squirrel has collected 8 acorns for the winter.

Mommy squirrel decides 8 acorns are not enough for her family. She collects 2 more. How many acorns does Mommy squirrel have now?

2 more than 8 is 10. Mommy squirrel now has 10 acorns.

# 2. One Less

Patrick loves to collect seashells. Let's find out how many he has collected.

6 seashells

Patrick has 6 seashells in his collection.

One shell fell down and broke.
Now Patrick has **1 less** seashell.

6 seashells | 1 less seashell | 5 seashells

1 less than 6 is 5. Patrick now has 5 seashells.

# Two Less

Look at these 5 frogs sitting on a log.

2 frogs jumped into the pond.

Count how many frogs are left on the log.

3 frogs

**3** frogs

2 less than 5 is 3. There are 3 frogs left on the log.

| **5** frogs | **2** less frogs | **3** frogs |
|---|---|---|

# 3. Equal To

Felicia and Sean are building towers with blocks. They want their towers to look the same. For that, both need to use the same number of blocks.

Felicia's tower is taller than Sean's.

5 is not the same as 3

**DID YOU KNOW?**

Equal means being the same in quantity or amount.

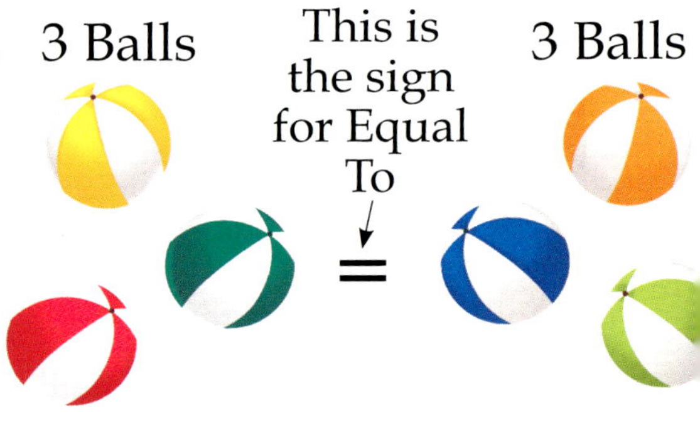

Sean adds 2 more blocks to make his tower equal to Felicia's.

5 is the same as 3 plus 2.

**POCKET FACT**

**3 blocks add two blocks equals to 5 blocks. We can say this in words, or use the signs + and = to write 3+2 = 5.**

# 4. Addition

1 more than 1 is 2.

1 more than 2 is 3.

1 more than 3 is 4.

This is addition. Adding means joining numbers to get a new total.

**POCKET FACT**

A **Sum** is the new number you get when you add numbers.

Count and find the new total on the number line:

5 + 1 = **6**

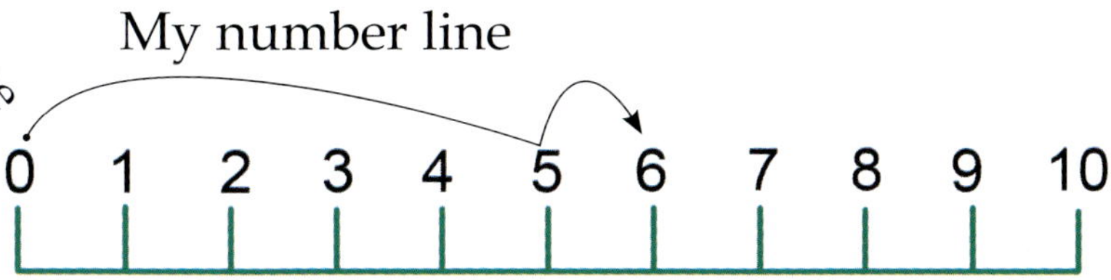


6 + 2 = **8**

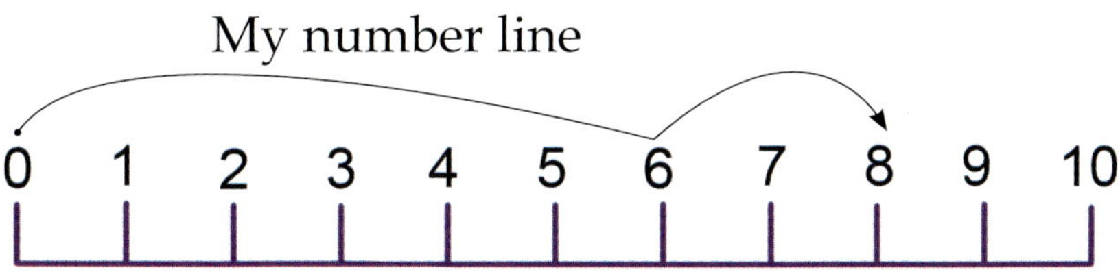


7 + 3 = **10**

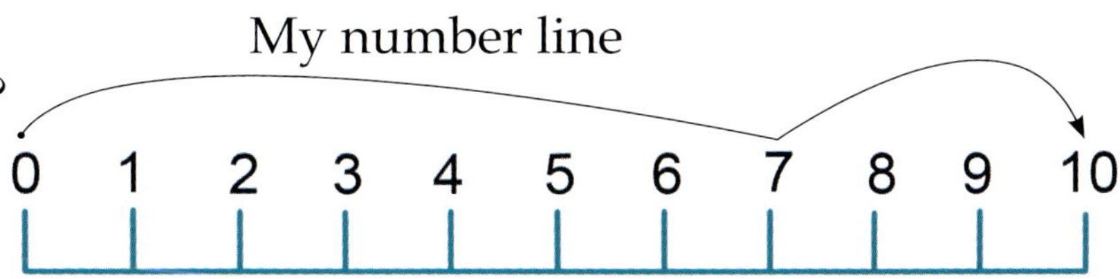


**DID YOU KNOW?**

This is the '**plus**' sign. It is a symbol to show addition.

# Adding with the Plus sign

A plus sign is used in place of the words 'add' or 'more'. It is a part of an addition problem. It helps to add numbers together.

10 flowers add 1 flower 11 flowers

13 cars add 1 car 14 cars

15 balls add 5 balls 20 balls

**POCKET FACT**

4+0=4

If you add zero to another number, the number does not change.

# 5. Subtraction

1 less than 5 is 4.

1 less than 4 is 3.

1 less than 3 is 2.

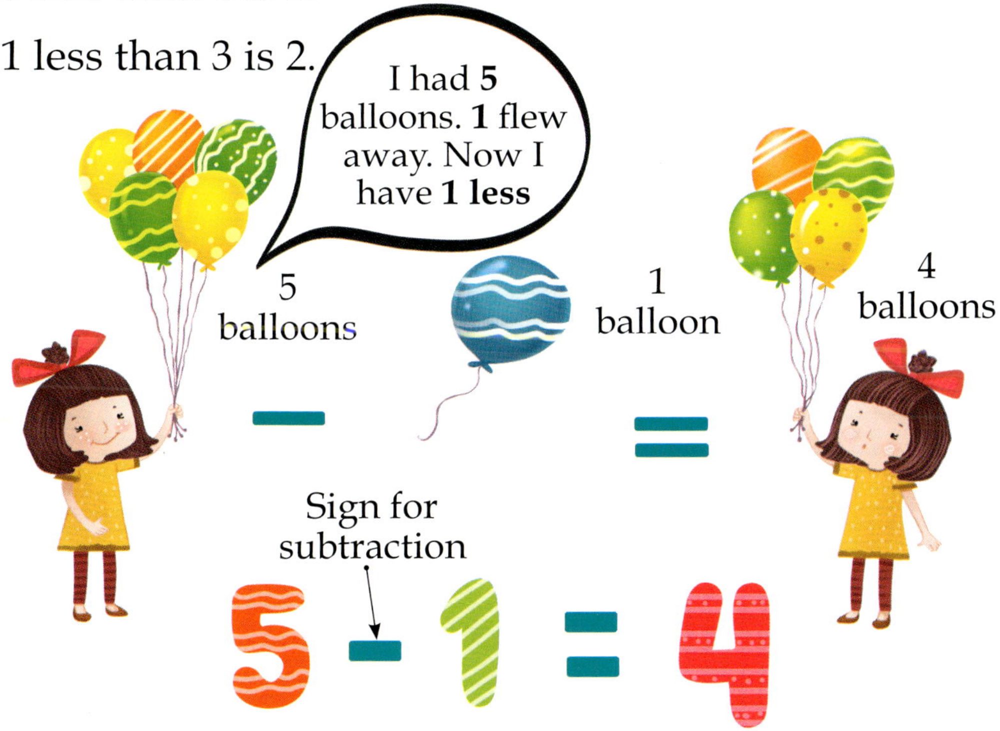


This is subtraction. Subtracting is the opposite of adding. It means to take away a number and finding what is left.

**POCKET FACT**

**Difference** is the number that is left when you subtract a number from another.

Count and find the result on the number line.

10 - 1 = **9**

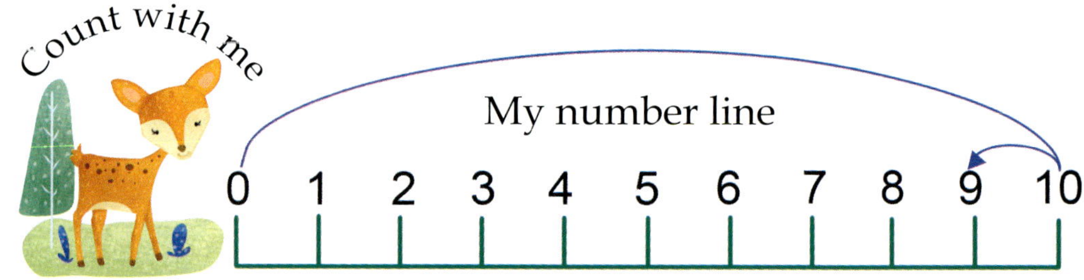


8 - 2 = **6**

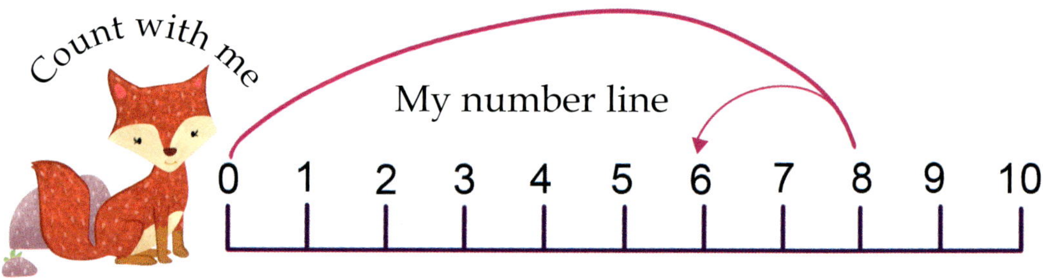


6 - 3 = **3**

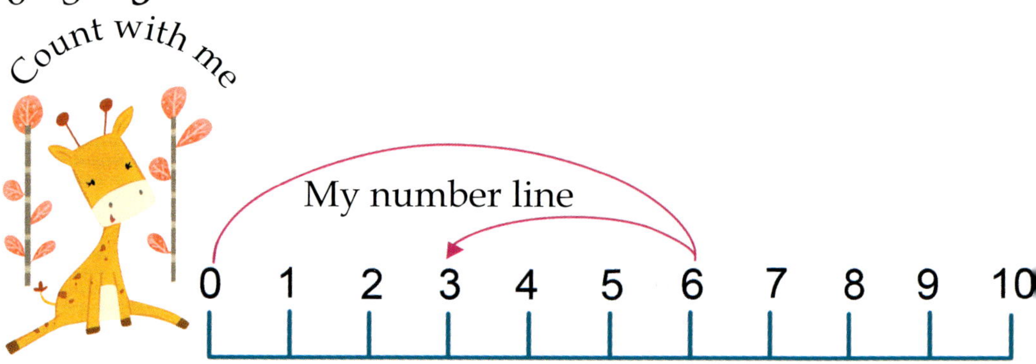

**POCKET FACT**

This is the **minus** sign. It is a symbol to show subtraction.

# Subtracting with the Minus sign

A minus sign is used in place of the words 'take away' and 'less'. It is a part of a subtraction problem. It helps to subtract one number from another.

 − subtract  = 

8 icecreams 1 icecream 7 icecreams

 − subtract  = 

13 ants 3 ants 10 ants

 − subtract  = 

6 apples 2 apples 4 apples

# 6. Number Names

## One to Five

| | | |
|---|---|---|
| 1 | ONE |  |
| 2 | TWO | 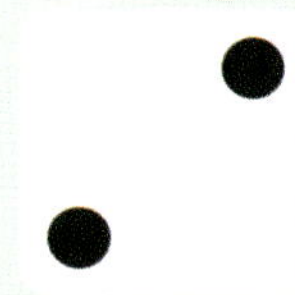 |
| 3 | THREE | 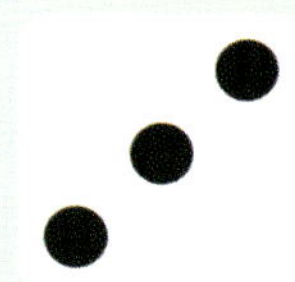 |
| 4 | FOUR | 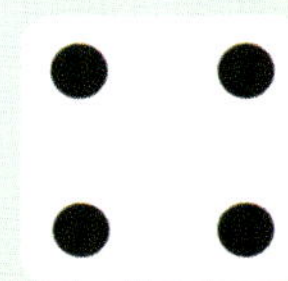 |
| 5 | FIVE | 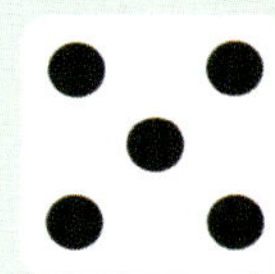 |

**POCKET FACT**

**Number names are numbers written in words.**

# Six to Ten

| | | |
|---|---|---|
| 6 | SIX |  |
| 7 | SEVEN |  |
| 8 | EIGHT | 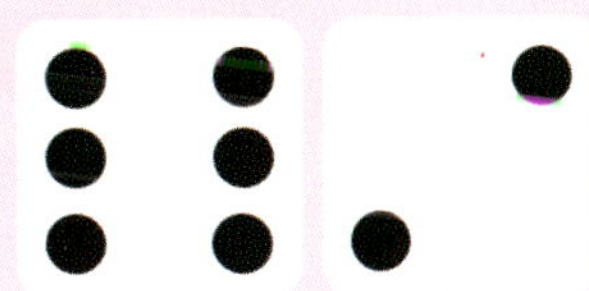 |
| 9 | NINE | 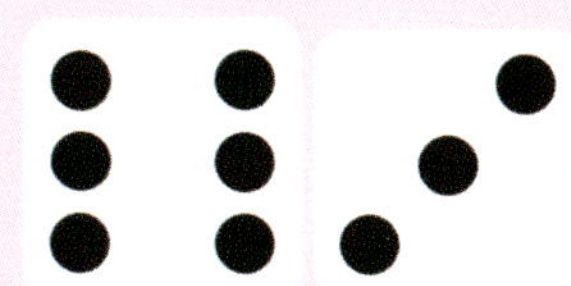 |
| 10 | TEN |  |

**DID YOU KNOW?**

All numbers from 10 to 99 are 2-digit numbers.

# 7. Story Problems

Stacy and her best friend Moe make a great team of 2.

Stacy has 2 dolls. Moe has 3. Together they have 5 lovely dolls to play with.

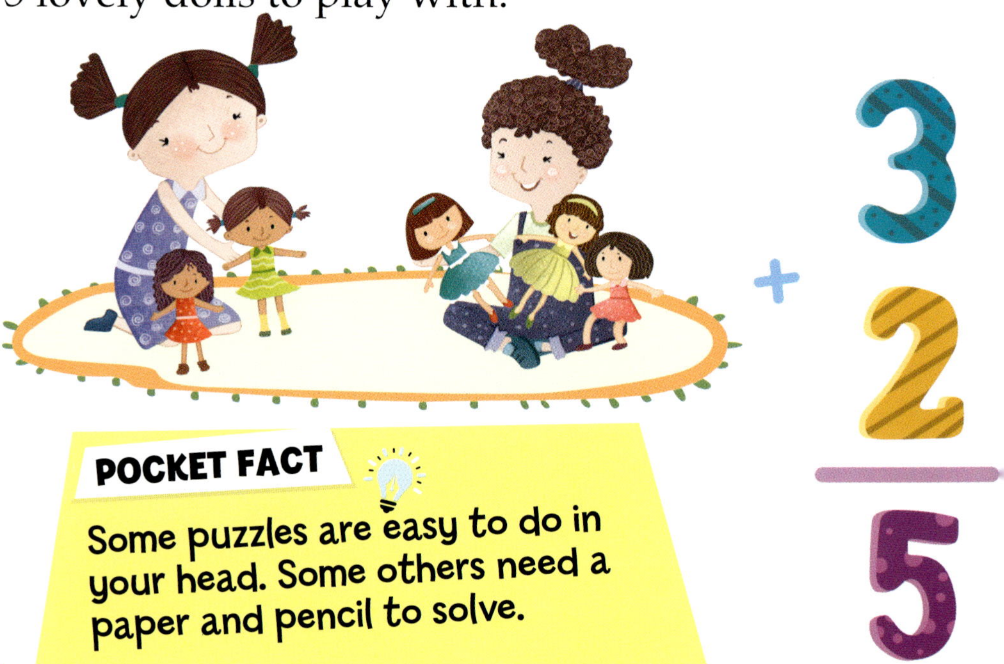


**POCKET FACT**

**Some puzzles are easy to do in your head. Some others need a paper and pencil to solve.**

Stacy's mother made them 5 pancakes each. 5 plus 5 equals 10 yummy pancakes.

$$5 + 5 = 10$$

Stacy's class at school has 9 girls and 10 boys. The sum of 9 and 10 is 19 smart children.

$$\begin{array}{r} 9 \\ +\,10 \\ \hline 19 \end{array}$$

**DID YOU KNOW?** Addition puzzles can be solved from left to right or top to bottom.

Peter's grandma baked 12 of Peter's favourite choco chip cookies. Peter took 5 away to eat. Seven cookies were left.

$$12 - 5 = 7$$

The apple tree in Peter's garden had 16 apples. Peter and his friends plucked 4 apples. 12 apples were left on the tree.

$$\begin{array}{r} 16 \\ -\ 4 \\ \hline 12 \end{array}$$

**POCKET FACT**

By subtracting, you can find the difference between the two numbers.

Peter blew 13 bubbles. 5 of them popped. How many bubbles remained?

13 minus 5 is 8. Eight bubbles remain.

$$\begin{array}{r} 13 \\ -\ 5 \\ \hline 8 \end{array}$$

Six birds were sitting on a tree branch. One flew away. Five birds stayed on the branch.

**DID YOU KNOW?**

Like addition, subtraction puzzles can be solved from left to right or top to bottom.

$$6 - 1 = 5$$

# Fun with Addition and Subtraction

(a) What is the sum of 3 blue flags and 3 red flags?

(b) I sold 10 popcorn bags in the morning and 10 in the evening. How many did I sell in total?

(c) The roller coaster has 10 seats. 9 people are riding it. How many seats are empty?

(d) I had 4 ice-creams in my hand. If 1 melted away in the sun, how many do I have left?

Let's Get Active

## Number Names

Circle the number names in the grid.

| ONE | TWO | THREE | FOUR | FIVE |
|---|---|---|---|---|
| SIX | SEVEN | EIGHT | NINE | TEN |

| H | N | R | F | Y | M | E | W | D |
|---|---|---|---|---|---|---|---|---|
| M | L | Q | U | T | B | Q | Y | U |
| N | I | N | E | K | T | S | Q | P |
| O | Z | O | N | E | W | E | D | C |
| I | S | V | X | I | O | V | P | Z |
| T | I | Z | C | G | T | E | N | S |
| G | X | E | N | H | M | N | Z | J |
| T | N | V | J | T | F | I | V | E |
| T | H | R | E | E | F | O | U | R |

## Circle the correct sum:

| | | | | |
|---|---|---|---|---|
|  | + |  | 5 | 6 |
| 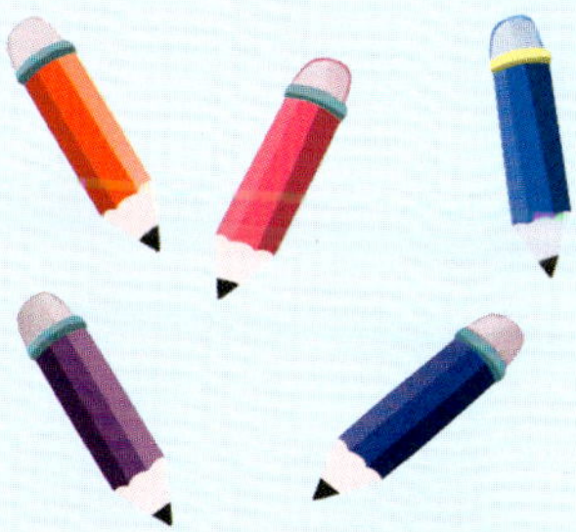 | + | 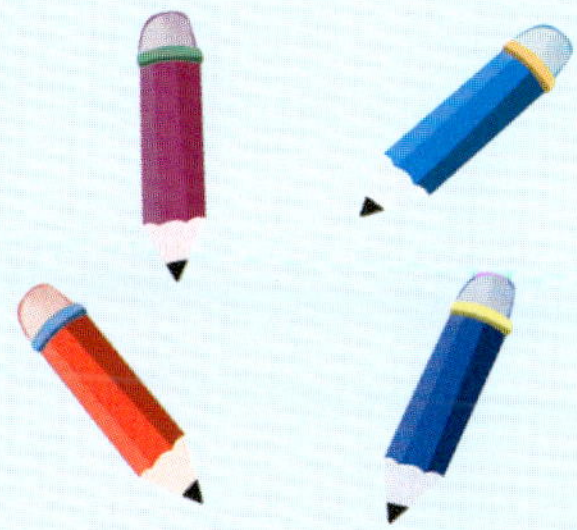 | 10 | 9 |
|  | + |  | 12 | 11 |
|  | + |  | 13 | 4 |

**Find the difference:**

Use the number line to solve the subtraction problems:

1. 3 -1 = _____

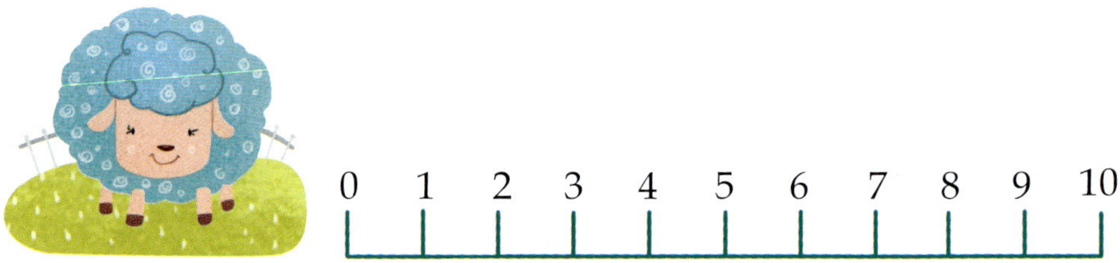


2. 6 - 2 = _____

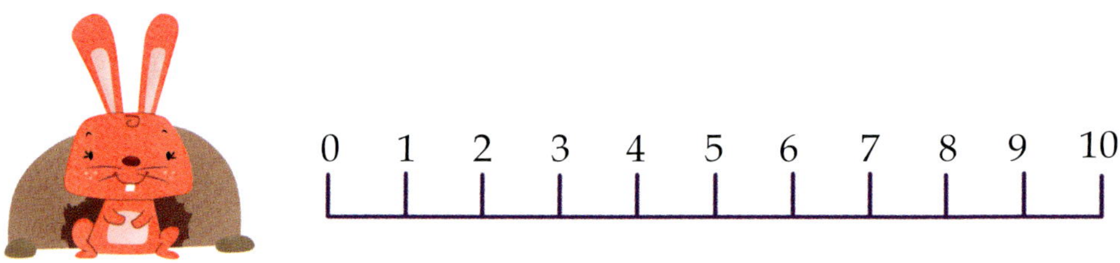


3. 10 - 5 = _____

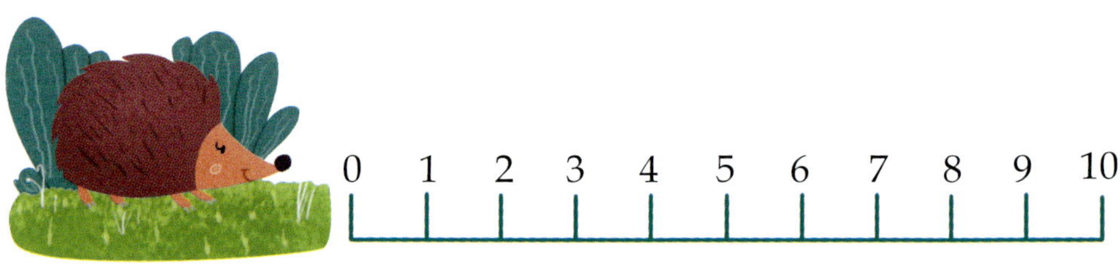


4. 9 - 3 = _____

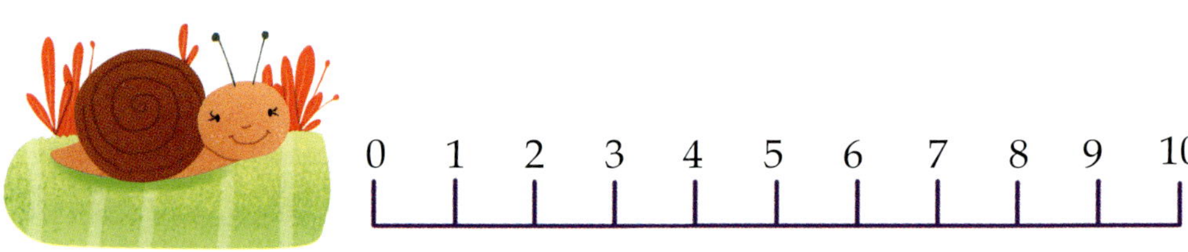

**Colour by numbers:**

Solve the addition and subtraction problems, then colour according to the number.

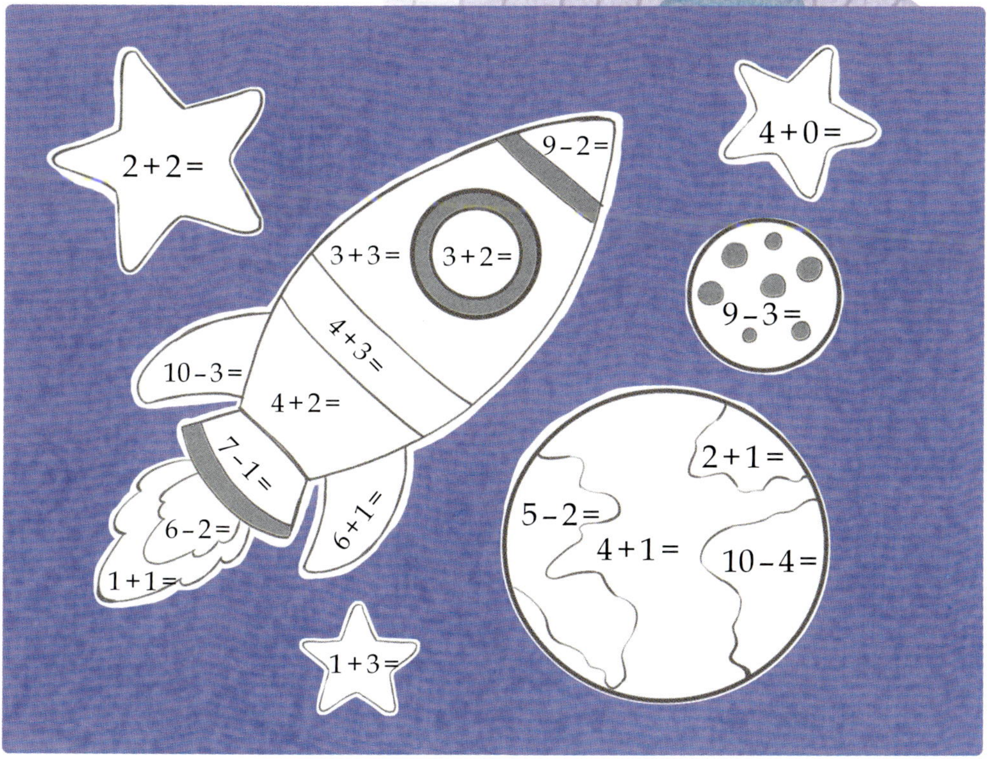

## GLOSSARY

| | |
|---|---|
| Add | to bring two or more numbers together to make a new total |
| Collect | to gather an accumulation of things especially as a hobby |
| Count | recite numbers in ascending order |
| Difference | the number that is left after subtracting one number from another |
| Equal | being the same in quantity, size, degree, or value |
| Less | to indicate a smaller amount of |
| Minus | used to indicate subtraction; short for minus sign |
| More | to indicate a greater amount of |
| Plus | used to indicate addition |
| Puzzle | a game, toy, or problem designed to test knowledge |
| Sell | give something in exchange for money |

## ANSWERS

Page 26-27. (a) 6 flags
(b) 20 popcorn bags
(c) 1 seat
(d) 3 icecreams

Page 28.

| | | | | | | | | |
|---|---|---|---|---|---|---|---|---|
| H | N | R | F | Y | M | E | W | D |
| M | L | Q | U | T | B | Q | Y | U |
| N | I | N | E | K | T | S | Q | P |
| O | Z | O | N | E | W | E | D | C |
| I | S | V | X | I | O | V | P | Z |
| T | I | Z | C | G | T | E | N | S |
| G | X | E | N | H | M | N | Z | J |
| T | N | V | J | T | F | I | V | E |
| T | H | R | E | E | F | O | U | R |

Page 29.

Page 30. 1. 2 2. 4
3. 5 4. 6

Page 31.

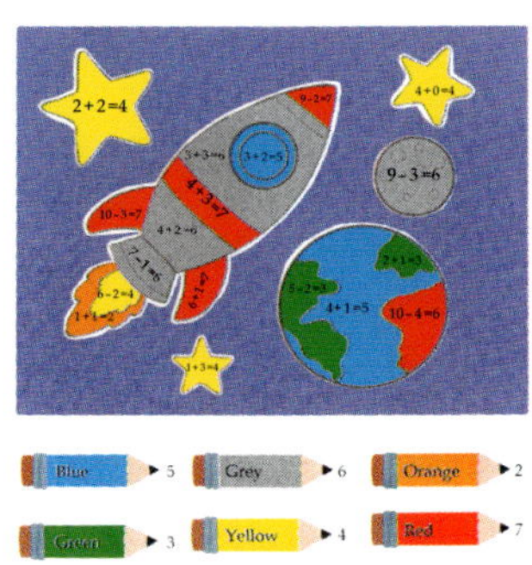